D0911018

A Miracle
for Your Marriage

by
John Osteen

Unless otherwise indicated, all Scripture quotations in this book are from the King James Version of the Bible.

Copyright © 1988 by John Osteen

ISBN 0-912631-38-4

Lakewood Church
P.O. Box 23297
Houston, Texas 77228

And the third day there was a marriage in Cana of Galilee; and the mother of Jesus was there: And both Jesus was called, and his disciples, to the marriage. And when they wanted wine, the mother of Jesus saith unto him, They have no wine. Jesus saith unto her, Woman, what have I to do with thee? mine hour is not yet come. His mother saith unto the servants, Whatsoever he saith unto you, do it.

And there were set there six waterpots of stone, after the manner of the purifying of the Jews, containing two or three firkins apiece. Jesus saith unto them, Fill the waterpots with water. And they filled them up to the brim. And he saith unto them, Draw out now, and bear unto the governor of the feast. And they bare it.

When the ruler of the feast had tasted the water that was made wine, and knew not whence it was: (but the servants which drew the water knew;) the governor of the feast called the bridegroom, and saith unto him, Every man at the beginning doth set forth good wine; and when men have well drunk, then that which is worse: but thou hast kept the good wine until now. This beginning of miracles did Jesus in Cana of Galilee, and manifested forth his glory; and his disciples believed on him (John 2:1-11).

A Miracle for Your Marriage

The devil is out to destroy your home.

He wants to destroy and divide every husband and wife.

Families are under attack, leaving husbands, wives, and little children wounded and scarred. Thousands of homes are disintegrating and falling apart.

It may be that you are having trouble in your marriage and in your home. Heartache and sorrow have moved in and taken up residence there. You've cried out to the Lord for an answer—for a miracle in your marriage. Well, thank God, Jesus Christ has an answer for you, for your hurting marriage. God can change your situation around and bring joy and happiness back to your home.

God has given us a great desire to help build and strengthen marriages and homes here at Lakewood Church. We need to bring healing and restoration to troubled and broken marriages. Good marriages need to be strengthened. People from all walks of life and from all denominations need help. We have seen many marriages healed and touched by the power of God. We believe the power of God is able to bring healing to your marriage, too.

God established the home first, even before He created the Church. And the devil knows if he can destroy the family unit that he can destroy much more beyond that. But aren't you glad God is in the restoration business? He is going to restore your home and your marriage and give a miracle to husbands and wives everywhere.

The first miracle

The turning of water into wine, was the first miracle Jesus ever performed. And this miracle has great significance.

Why was the wedding being held in a home? What was Jesus trying to tell us through this miracle? He wasn't just turning water into wine. That wasn't the important thing. No, some deeper truth is to be found here. God wants us to understand that His miracle power can change things!

Jesus changed water into wine but He can change far more than that. He can change things in your home, or even change the people. He can change a husband, He can change a wife, He can change you and make you a totally new person. If you are a born-again believer, you have been changed by the power of God. The Bible says, *Therefore if any man be in Christ, he is a new creature: old things are passed away; behold, all things are become new* (2 Corinthians 5:17).

Perhaps your husband is an alcoholic. Maybe your wife left you. Maybe you are on the verge of divorce. God can change all that. He can turn your situation around and bring healing to you, your mate, and your marriage.

Is your husband or your wife unsaved? God will deliver that unsaved mate and make a new creature out of them. The Word of God says, *The Lord is...not willing that any should perish, but that all* [that includes your mate!] *should come to repentance* (2 Peter 3:9). God hasn't given up on the human race, so don't you dare give up on your mate!

If you don't like your wife, God can give you a *new* one. Now, don't throw this book against the wall—hear me out. I don't mean that He will bring someone new into your life so you can get a divorce. God will use His miracle-working power and change the wife you've got. If you don't like your husband, He will give you a new husband by making him over again. Jesus is the Miracle-Worker, the Son of the Living God, and He changes people, He changes circumstances.

You may be saying, "I'm between a rock and a hard place. An impenetrable wall is before me. There is no way out." I don't claim to have all the answers but I know that Jesus is the One who can change that situation just like He did for this couple:

We were married on September 15, 1984. Prior to this we had been in full-time ministry work. During the time that we were in the ministry, the leaders announced to us if we were to get married, our marriage would not last three years. We went into our marriage with this

9

weighing heavy on our hearts. After two-and-a-half years into our marriage, the prophecy we had been told seemed to be coming true. We drifted further apart from each other and God until the day my husband announced to me that he wanted a divorce.

At first, my world was shattered and all hope was gone. Then at a Bible Study, I was given information on Lakewood Church. I attended the services and hope was restored. My faith grew and I began to see that it was God's will for my marriage to be restored.

In the natural, things got worse. But I pressed on in with the Word of God, and in prayer. I knew the gates of hell could not stand against God's Word. On March 29, 1987, my husband announced to me that he was coming home. Since then, our marriage has been strengthened and our love has been rekindled. We give God all the glory because we know that His Word does not return void but accomplishes that which it is sent out to perform!

Jesus goes to weddings

Jesus visits marriages. He makes it a point to go to weddings, and He watches out for couples. He sees the sorrow, the heartaches, and the joy. He sees children and how they will be affected by a home that's ripped apart at the seams by strife and divorce.

Mark 10:6-9 says, *But from the beginning of the creation God made them male and female. For this cause shall a man leave his father and mother, and cleave to his wife; And they twain shall be one flesh:*

so then they are no more twain, but one flesh. What therefore God hath joined together, let not man put asunder.

God loves you. He does not want you to get a divorce and break up your home. You may be involved in an adulterous relationship, or drugs, or alcohol. God wants you to be free from these things. Jesus can give you power over the devil (see Luke 10:19) who drives you to commit adultery, to drink, or to take drugs. You can be free. You can have a home that cannot be destroyed because it's founded upon the Rock, Christ Jesus (see Matthew 7:24-27).

A couple in our church had their marriage healed several years ago. The husband didn't know Jesus and he got into adultery and became an alcoholic. He left his wife when they had two children and she was expecting another child.

She began to pray for him day and night. She stood faithfully on Mark 11:24, *Therefore I say unto you, What things soever ye desire, when ye pray, believe that ye receive them, and ye shall have them.* Her husband told her that he didn't want to have anything to do with her and that he wanted her to leave him alone. But she refused to be moved by circumstances, by what her husband said and did. She just kept praying the Word of God over him.

One day God touched this man's heart and he returned home to his family. After they were reunited, he accepted Jesus and received the baptism in the Holy Ghost! Today this couple is helping minister to other hurting marriages and encouraging mates to believe God for their families to be restored.

This husband wrote me a letter:

Thank God for your words of encouragement and teachings on marriage restoration and healing.

My marriage was healed because my wife refused to believe the lies of the devil, choosing rather to believe God and trust Him. As she allowed God to work in her life she began to pray and rely upon the Word of God. Her prayers and the power of God set me free from alcoholism, adultery, addiction to gambling, and brought me home to my family. It was a miracle! Praise You, Jesus.

The teaching of the Word of God and putting Scriptures to work in our lives has really helped our marriage grow. We are even able to help other marriages through the teachings at Lakewood Church. Thanks again, Pastor. We love you.

Power to rise above the natural

The miracle at Cana also demonstrates that Jesus, using His miracle power, can rise above the natural laws of what our minds can comprehend.

You see, water is supposed to stay water. All the water I've ever seen has never changed into anything else. But Jesus is not limited to man's ability.

You may say, "No man can help me." But the things that are impossible with man are possible with God (see Matthew 19:26). They are possible—now get this, this is important—*if we get* **with God.** If you are just with man all the time, then it's impossible. Get away from man and *get with God.* With God, all things are possible.

Maybe you're reading this book and saying to yourself, *Yes, Brother Osteen, but you don't know how bad it is at my house. I don't see how my marriage could ever be repaired. I don't know how it could ever be healed. I don't know how this situation could ever be worked out.* Well, just remember this: with man it's impossible, but not with God.

God is a God who can do the impossible! He can heal you of all the hurts and wounds of the past. You don't have to live with a broken heart. Luke 4:18 says Jesus came to heal the brokenhearted. Psalm 147:3 says that He binds up wounds. The Lord is concerned about you and definitely is interested in the healing of your home. Let Him heal your broken heart so you can have healing in your marriage. The following letter is a testimony to this truth:

I left my husband on October 2, because I gave up. I kept telling myself, "You are better off single." I told myself over and over we did not love each other any more, and that only some things can be forgiven. I got to where I dreaded going home for fear of the fighting.

I packed all my things and left before my husband came home from work. I really thought that was what he wanted. We were constantly arguing and fighting. We hit each other and hurt each other. There was so much bitterness and unforgiveness from the past. We really felt we had lost love for each other.

After I left, I decided to go to a service at Lakewood Church in hopes of getting some answers for myself. My husband was so bitter he wouldn't even speak to me. He said the only way I could ever come back would be on his terms.

The thing he never understood is that you can't make somebody change. They have to have the desire in their heart. Only God can put that desire there. He did for me.

At Lakewood Church, I learned for the first time what marriage was all about. I asked the Lord to change what needed to be changed and He immediately took over. God is so good. All I had to do was ask! The things I wanted my husband to change naturally took place when I made the initial change myself.

I called my husband again and asked him to please come the following week. I went to see him and poured my heart out to him. For the first time in ages we communicated. I watched the bitterness fall off his face. God was really working that day. My husband was suddenly willing to work with me and our marriage. I admitted all my faults and did not care about his for the first time.

The Lord has healed me of all bitterness. My family is now living for the Lord and all of us are going to Lakewood Church. It is something I never thought I would see and now it has come to pass!

The devil has come to steal and to kill and to destroy your marriage. Marriage was meant to have life, and life more abundantly. Your marriage may seem dead, but God can give it life. Jesus said, *I am come that they might have life, and that they might have it more abundantly* (John 10:10).

God gave us an example in the Old Testament of His ability to overcome natural circumstances by His miracle-working power. God took two million people through the wilderness for 40 years—there were no drug stores, no doctors, no lawyers, no housing units, no grocery stores, and yet God took care of the Israelites.

He provided clothes that wouldn't wear out, and shoes that wouldn't wear out. When they needed water, it came out of a rock. And when they needed food, it rained down from heaven. You see, God is not limited to our ability. The Bible says, *God shall supply all your need according to his riches in glory by Christ Jesus* (Philippians 4:19).

Jesus took five loaves of bread and two little fishes and, rising above the natural laws, fed a multitude. If Jesus did miracles then, He can do miracles for you! He's the same yesterday, today, and forever (see Hebrews 13:8). Time and time again, He has demonstrated His power to rise above the natural into the supernatural.

Do you have an emergency, right now? Is it a crisis? Maybe it's a physical, spiritual, or financial crisis. Is there a crisis with your home, your children, your husband, your wife? You see, Jesus was there when the crisis came up at the wedding in Cana. He was in that home, at the wedding. And He is there for your crisis time. He has not taken His eyes off you.

I encourage you to look to Jesus today. You've looked to drugs. You've looked to alcohol, to liquor, to wine. You've looked to adultery. You've looked to playing the field and all of that. You've looked everywhere but to Jesus. And Jesus is your Answer. You need to look to Him.

A couple who came to Lakewood Church testifies to that fact:

Our marriage did not have a good start. We did not know God, nor His plan of salvation for our lives. Destructive emotions, lack of self-confidence, and distrust almost killed our marriage. My husband felt insecure and was very jealous and at times, violent. This jealousy brought fear into our marriage. My husband's lack of trust in me made me feel like a prisoner.

We loved each other very much, but something was missing in our marriage. A wall began to build up between us—a wall of resentment, anger, strife, bitterness, and eventually hate. Fifteen years passed by and we were both suffering tremendously. We knew we needed help but did not know where to turn. We tried to find help in the world through family counseling, and even started attending a denominational church, but this was not the answer. We did not know that in Jesus there is love, joy, peace, and happiness. It seemed that we had no hope.

But one day, God, in His tender mercy and love reached down and touched my husband. He received deliverance immediately from the spirit of jealousy. Praise God! Within a week our whole family was saved.

Four months after our salvation, God placed us at Lakewood ("An Oasis of Love"). We found the Word of God being preached, shown, and lived. We began to study God's

Word, which caused us to grow spiritually. In the Word, we learned about God's promises and how to be an overcomer—how to stand on the Word of God and how to take a stand against the devil. Through the Word we became closer to God and closer to each other.

We are so glad God laid it on our hearts to begin attending Lakewood Church several months ago. We have a strong desire to learn more about God's plan for happier marriages, and since He has blessed us we have a burden to help others who are having marital problems. We can testify that God is the Answer to all problems, and that there is no happiness outside of God. God ordained marriage, and He wants the best for us.

Through the help we received at Lakewood Church we are able to tell and share with others how God is truly a Healer, and how He can restore families back together.

The end of man's limitations

At the wedding in Cana, Jesus demonstrated His power to work a miracle when man had come to the end of his limit. That's very important. When the servants summoned Jesus, they had come face-to-face with their limitations. The wine had run out. But Jesus demonstrated His power to work at the end of man's limitations.

Someone once said man's extremity is God's opportunity. And you may already be at your extremity. But where your power ends, Jesus' power begins.

17

Look at this dramatic testimony. It took this husband coming to the end of himself before he would reach out to God:

Just over a year ago my wife left me. She took our two boys and moved out. I had come to the end of myself. I was nearly destroyed by this work of the devil, but when I cried out to God, He honored my prayers and began to bless me.

Believing for the healing of my marriage was the toughest fight I've ever gone through, but praise God, after many, many miraculous things, my wife agreed to come back to me.

I want to thank you because when I wrote you, you sent me some wonderful encouragement and Scriptures when most everybody else told me to give up. Thank you!

When they ran out of wine at the wedding in Cana, Jesus did not arrogantly walk up to the servants and say, "I'll do it all. You just sit down and don't think about it anymore. I'm a mighty Miracle-Worker." Instead, He asked them to do what they could. He told them to fill the pots with water so that He would be able to do what they couldn't do. He asked them to do the possible in order that He might do the impossible. He asked them to do the natural in order that He might do the supernatural.

You see, many times we want our marriages healed and we say, "God, You just do it all. Here I am. If You want to do anything about it, just do it." Or, "If God wants our marriage to work, just let Him work a miracle." But the Lord doesn't work that way. The Lord expects us to do what we can do. The Lord expects us to do the possible. The Lord expects us to do what we can do in the natural.

"What can I do?" you ask. You can forgive. You can go the extra mile. You can get up and write that letter. You can make that telephone call. You can make that move. You can admit that you were wrong. You can confess your sins (see James 5:16). You can release bitterness and anger from your heart (see Ephesians 4:31,32). You can overcome evil with good (see Romans 12:21). You can ask God to show you how to be a better husband or wife. You can pray and intercede for your mate until you see them delivered.

If you'll do the possible, Jesus will do the impossible. If you'll do what you can do, Jesus will do what you can't do. If you'll do the natural, Jesus will do the supernatural.

One husband and wife who came to Lakewood Church were both Spirit-filled Christians and working busily in the ministry. They knew the Word but they opened the door for the devil in their home. The husband wrote his story:

Four years ago, I left my wife. Though we were both saved and Spirit-filled Christians, I had allowed Satan to destroy our marriage by refusing to deal with our problems. Instead, I ran to drinking and a nightlife that God had previously delivered me from. Within a short while, I became involved in several adulterous affairs. I was spending a great deal of money that I did not really have by charging up credit cards

19

and obtaining several major bank loans. All of this was hidden from my wife.

As things grew worse and the truth about my life surfaced, the results were devastating. Any contact my wife and I had resulted in strife and confusion. She was very hurt as I continued in my sin. We lost our love for one another and saw divorce as the only answer.

After the divorce, we decided to each go on our separate ways. My wife continued to serve the Lord as I grew deeper into sin. I found myself without any peace and almost no fellowship with the Lord. I then felt that if I would only remarry, all my problems would be over. I began to make plans with a woman I was dating to do just that.

Unknown to me, during this same time, God had dealt with my wife. While attending the Lakewood Ladies Convention, God had spoken to her through Isaiah 55:8,9. The Lord said that His thoughts were that He could heal her marriage if she would pray and believe. She had received this as from the Lord and had taken a position of faith that God would deliver me and restore our marriage.

As I continued to make plans to remarry, I began to ask God to bless this marriage I was about to enter. Deep down inside I had no peace about this second marriage and I knew it was not the answer. Yet I continued to ask God's blessing. Not hearing from God on the upcoming marriage, I found myself really frustrated. I finally cried out to the Lord and asked Him to have His will be done in my life. That night I really began to seek the Lord. The Holy Spirit led me to a set of your tapes, titled "Thinking the Thoughts of God." I listened to them all night as they really ministered to me. That night I found myself broken and repentant before God. I knew I had heard from Him. I found His forgiveness and love. I also received wisdom and strength from Him to do His will.

The next morning, I knew what I had to do. I called the woman I was about to marry and called off the wedding. I then went to the minister who was to marry us and I told him what had happened. He advised me to follow God and prayed with me that God would heal my marriage. I then went to see my wife and shared what I had gone through that night. She told me how that she had taken a stand and had been praying and believing God to deliver me. We prayed and agreed that God would restore our marriage.

We began to attend Lakewood Church regularly. There, we found love and healing for all of our past hurts. Almost a year later, we were remarried. Thank you for teaching the Word of God and for extending His love and forgiveness to us.

The Lord Jesus wants to heal marriages. He wants to restore what the devil has stolen and destroyed. Many times the devil gets in and makes people mad. Then they get bitter, angry, and hurt. People have said to me, "My husband is the one who is in the wrong. He committed adultery!"

Do you know how I answer? "God forgave you, why don't you forgive your mate? God is a God of mercy. God has forgiven you and will continue to forgive you. Why don't you forgive?" Jesus forgave the woman caught in adultery and He is our example (see John 8:3-11).

How tragic it is for homes to be destroyed, for husbands and wives to be torn apart. Divorce is not your answer. It does a terrible injustice to little boys and little girls. It tears their hearts and their lives apart, leaving them scarred for life. Don't do that to your children. Don't do that to your home. Rise up. If you will do what you can do, God will do what you can't do. *This is the hour for the healing of your home and the healing of your marriage!*

Love never fails

There's not a couple alive on this earth who hasn't experienced trouble in their marriage at some point in time. Dodie and I were married for at least a couple of weeks before we had trouble!

When we first got married Dodie couldn't cook a lick. I don't know whether you can cook licks or not but she couldn't cook. She couldn't fry water. I almost starved to death! I ate out for several weeks without telling her. She just couldn't cook!

But oh how she could love! It's not whether you burn the toast and offer a burnt offering to your husband every morning! No, love is what counts. If you love, that love will never fail. The devil wants to make you think you've lost love for your mate, but it has just been buried by hurts from your relationship. Let God uncover that love. He will if you ask Him to.

22

Read this beautiful testimony of how God did just that:

We have been married almost 10 years—we have five children and are enjoying what God has done for us. When we got married we were both saved, Spirit filled, and serving the Lord, but the day we got married went from the happiest to the saddest in just a few hours. The next two to three years we went through hell in our marriage. The night of our honeymoon things were said and done that were so damaging to our relationship that few people would have stayed together. So much hurt and bitterness developed that it made it almost impossible to communicate without arguing. We fought all the time—even physically. The first two years of our marriage we did not enjoy one happy day of marriage.

During this time of crisis we started to attend Lakewood Church, and sat under your teaching and other well-known leaders in the Body of Christ. The only time we could get along was when we were at church.

We began to learn about the Word of God and what actually belonged to us because of what Jesus did at Calvary. The main truth that set us free was the authority we have over demon powers—we were completely ignorant of Satan and demon powers and how they operate. The Bible clearly tells us that the thief—Satan—comes to steal, kill, and destroy—that's what was happening to our marriage.

We got married because we loved each other and wanted to serve the Lord together, and the devil hates that. He created a negative atmosphere around us through feelings, emotions, and words and then we acted on it, and it produced nothing but death in our marriage. The Bible says in the tongue is the power of death and life—we didn't know that at the time we got married every negative thing that we said was bringing death to our marriage. The devil was using it to destroy us, but praise God, we found the truth.

As the husband, I would submit to God by doing and acting what the Bible said to do instead of letting the feelings and emotions to strike out against my wife dictate to me. When anger would come, I would say, "No you don't devil—I resist you and I will not act with the emotion of anger but instead I will be kind and love my wife and make myself act according to the Bible." I had lost all love for my wife, but learning these truths, I began to confess that I loved my wife and said it to her over and over again when my inward feeling was hate for her.

By calling things that be not as though they were (Romans 4:17), I changed the way I felt about my wife. Love again began to be created inside of me for her by my willingly saying it out of my mouth. The devil is a thief and he stole our love, but through knowledge of the Word of God and by acting on it regardless of how we felt, we took it all back out of the devil's hands—praise the Lord! This took place over a three-year period—it took time, patience, and endurance, but the Bible says we are not weak but strong.

Thanks for your uncompromising stand on the Word of God and your faithfulness to teach it to those who will hear. God bless you.

Love like God loves

You see, we need to demonstrate our love to each other. One word of caution: Many husbands and wives get into a dangerous area when they start holding themselves from each other physically—going around in a huff and punishing their mate by holding the sexual relationship from them. The Bible says, *Let the husband render unto the wife due benevolence: and likewise also the wife unto the husband. Defraud ye not one the other, except it be with consent for a time, that ye may give yourselves to fasting and prayer* (1 Corinthians 7:3,5). The sexual relationship is not to be used as a tool. God commands us to be happily joined together. And God wants us to be lovers because love never fails.

Once when Dodie and I were dating, we were sitting outside just enjoying the brilliance of a full moon. I was looking at Dodie and she was looking at me. I said, "Oh, Dodie, how I love you. I tell you I love you. I wish I had a thousand arms to hug you with!"

Dodie turned to me and said, "I'm not interested in what you would do with a thousand arms. What are you going to do with the two you've got?" We must learn to demonstrate our love to our mate—every day!

You have the potential and ability to love like God loves. Roman 5:5 says that God has poured out

His love in your heart by the Holy Spirit. First Corinthians 13 is the great love chapter of the Bible. You need to practice walking in love toward your mate.

You can begin by confessing:

I endure long and I am patient and kind to my mate.

I am never envious or boil over with jealousy.

I am not boastful or vainglorious.

I do not display myself haughtily.

I am not conceited, arrogant, or inflated with pride.

I am not rude or unmannerly.

I do not act unbecomingly.

I do not insist on my own rights or my own way, for I am not self-seeking.

I am not touchy or fretful or resentful.

I take no account of an evil done to me; I pay no attention to a suffered wrong.

I do not rejoice at injustice and unrighteousness, but I rejoice when right and truth prevail.

I bear up under anything and everything that comes.

I am ever ready to believe the best of my mate.

My hopes are fadeless under all circumstances.

I endure everything without weakening.

God's love in me never fails; never fades out, becomes obsolete, or comes to an end.

1 Corinthians 13:4-8
(Amplified Bible)

Jesus can help your marriage

The important thing the miracle at Cana shows us is Jesus' ability to help a marriage in trouble. He changed water into wine, but that's insignificant as far as we're concerned. He was changing *things*. He was demonstrating by His presence that He was interested in marriages, interested in what happens between couples.

He was there when you took your wedding vows. He was there when you said, "I do." He heard you say, "Until death do us part." In fact, Malachi 2:14 says that He was a witness on your wedding day. He was there and He has not forsaken you! You may be in trouble, but Jesus is still there. Divorce is not the answer. Look to Jesus.

If you are facing a crisis in your marriage, you need wisdom for your particular situation. You may be separated from your mate already or even facing divorce procedures. Your circumstances may seem insurmountable at this time. You need help, you need answers. I have good news...there are answers.

James 1:5 says, *If any of you lack wisdom, let him ask of God, that giveth to all men liberally, and upbraideth not; and it shall be given him*. It does not say, "If you lack wisdom, call for your pastor, your friends, or a counselor." It says to ask God who gives liberally. He will tell you what to do, why you have turmoil in your marriage, and how you can change your situation. He will give *you* wisdom. He gets down to the nitty-gritty of life.

It's easy to run back and forth to people asking for answers when you're upset. But when you get with God, He knows your downsitting and uprising. He knows your thoughts afar off and not a word is on your tongue He doesn't know (see Psalm 139:2-4). Your Heavenly Father knows all about you. He knows what it will take to bring your mate home. He knows how to turn your situation around.

You don't have to lose your mate or your home. But you are going to have to be pushed into the presence of God. You must make time to seek the face of God. Jeremiah 33:3 is one of my favorite scriptures: *Call unto me, and I will answer thee, and shew thee great and mighty things, which thou knowest not.* The devil will do everything he can to keep you from seeking God, but you must put God first.

You may not know how to get your marriage healed, but God does. He loves *you*. He wants to talk to *you*. Read His Word and fellowship daily with Him in prayer. He knows how to do the impossible.

God created marriage and He knows how to make it work. He is a Miracle-Worker and He will work a miracle for your marriage!

What God has done for other restored marriages He will do for yours. It may be that you need to be saved. It may be that you need to just come back to God. I don't know the condition you're in, but God does. I want to pray with you and believe God with you for your marriage. Pray this prayer with me out loud right now:

"Father, I come to You in the Name of the Lord Jesus Christ, and in behalf of my home that is so torn with strife and heartache. Jesus, I'm asking for a miracle for my marriage. Mend our broken hearts and put our lives back together again. Restore the love we had for one another at the beginning and make it stronger than before."

Now let me pray for you:

Father, in Jesus' Name, I pray that you will touch this husband and wife. It may be that they are miles apart. Oh, God, help this husband to make a move. Help this wife to make a move. Help them, O God, in Jesus' Name to be merciful and forgiving…to get bitterness out of their hearts. I rebuke you, Satan, and I command you in the Name of Jesus Christ to take your hands off this family, this husband, this wife, these children. In the Name of Jesus Christ I charge you to go now. I release them from your hold. I believe the healing of their home and the healing of their marriage starts now, in Jesus' Name. Amen.

BOOKS BY JOHN OSTEEN

A Miracle For Your Marriage
Believing God For Your Loved Ones
* Healed of Cancer *by Dodie Osteen*
* How To Claim the Benefits of the Will
How To Demonstrate Satan's Defeat
How To Flow in the Super Supernatural
How To Release the Power of God
Overcoming Hindrances to Receiving the Baptism in the
    Holy Spirit
Overcoming Opposition: How To Succeed in Doing the
    Will of God *by Lisa Comes*
* Pulling Down Strongholds
Reigning in Life as a King
Rivers of Living Water
* Six Lies the Devil Uses to Destroy Marriages
    by Lisa Comes
The Believer's #1 Need
The Bible Way to Spiritual Power
The Confessions of a Baptist Preacher
* The Divine Flow
* The 6th Sense...Faith
The Truth Shall Set You Free
* There Is a Miracle in Your Mouth
This Awakening Generation
Unraveling the Mystery of the Blood Covenant
What To Do When the Tempter Comes
You Can Change Your Destiny
(continued next page)

Minibooks

A Place Called There
ABC's of Faith
Deception! Recognizing True and False Ministries
Four Principles in Receiving From God
How To Minister Healing to the Sick
* How To Receive Life Eternal
Keep What God Gives
Love & Marriage
* Receive the Holy Spirit
Saturday's Coming
Seven Facts About Prevailing Prayer
Seven Qualities of a Man of Faith
Spiritual Food For Victorious Living
* What To Do When Nothing Seems to Work

* Selected titles also available in Spanish

For a complete list of prices in the John Osteen Faith Library, please write to:

Lakewood Church
P.O. Box 23297
Houston, Texas 77228